SOUND/CHEST
AMISH TRIVEDI

ANNUAL
BOOKS

ANNUAL BOOKS
COVEN PRESS, LLC
Birmingham, Alabama
covenpress.com

Edited and designed by Jessica Smith, François Luong and
Gillian Devereux
Text: Adobe Garamond Pro
Titles: Myriad Pro

Cover image: "Empty card catalog" by Sage Ross
Used under a Creative Commons Attribution-Share Alike
license; cropped; © Sage Ross 2008
ragesoss.com

Library of Congress Cataloging-in-Publication Data

Trivedi, Amish, 1982—
Sound/Chest / Amish Trivedi
Annual Books #1
ISBN 13: 978-0692346266 (pbk. : alk. paper)
811.6—DC23

For Jennifer

TABLE OF CONTENTS

I like it when you're silent because it's like you're not there.
Pablo Neruda

જાગ્યા ત્યારથી સવાર
Jagya tyarathi savar
It's morning whenever you wake up.
Gujarati Saying

SOUND/CHEST

CLUSTERED/BRAIN   1728

After so many feet
of rising water,
what isn't tied up

in resistance
is tied up
in facts. My

favorite airbrush
is napalm. The
hours and
war: all

massacres
postponed. This national
plant is eroding into
skeletons and aspartame.
No one's angle
is their own and

I'm grinding
salt into your shoulders. The
print negatives are
grazing color.

A consciousness is unprepared
to be crushed into
dust. I didn't
want to torture them
like that. My new skin

plummeting and the discography
paint. Universes are bullet-
riddled and glorious, but
where did they go? To gaze
at milk: to hold out
for more splinters: washing
the dashboard, I found

teeth and a pair of pine
needles. Trouble is the only word
I can type with arrhythmia. I
saw a clavicle represented by
a two-tongued catastrophe and the
lights kept buzzing
to the room below. The grates were

holding the streets together, I'm
pretty sure. I don't follow

CELL/ATTRACTIVE   1739

My timing is the other wall:
a place for chairs and
osmosis to collect and
follow through. If there
were something so good,
I'd have destroyed it by
now. Whatever becomes
this membrane must be
preserved for nothing
but dust. At this time,
they've considered it
drowning and without
any sort of wind, we'll
end up against some
rocks, I guess. Something
like that, anyways.

This is the bread-basket
of print generation: the dots
are specs of motion. Every
copy I've seen reminds me
of a long about-face
in which I've seen a car
become a puncture of space. I've
lost a lot of blood here and
there up on the wall, but
the floors are bare
and brushed. If I
had another
set of lungs, I wouldn't
breathe with these
anymore.

A new, lovely way
to say "mistake." I should
have imagined these
bindings before. The moment
after must have been
amazing, but there's no
way to draw it out
or pretend it sprung up. This
last note is the orbit
of decay: please press
these stains to my face.
Anything included
in the sunset is mantra
and I felt out of it some
time back. These were
the same eyes that saw
what wasn't there, and
now all I want is the
vision—the way things
should have gone.

Crimes of humanity
is how the riot starts
and this is the decade
we are in. I have the
slow nitrates of Easter
and the handles are
going to come off. Every
surface feels like it was
sticky before this moment.

These veins,
my version of
anti-freeze. Like a
joker, I got mixed up
in the rackets
and forced

out of the deck. My disease in
grenadine and
your grandmother

has it out for me. I

built a house from
Bibles and glue sticks
so I could get high.
What Narcissus saw
in the water:
frustration and
taxes. All the trouble

you're in is the
fault of unborn
children who must
be punished. I've made up my
mind about
California: this time

I'm rescuing
skin cells. Before,
I was lying: you are the design.
You know the words I use—
these are not them, but
tangential. I've been blinded

by alabaster skin
or foils. Another reason
for discretion is anemia.
You talk like a horse
about mollusks and
all the parades quit
due to outpourings
of sunlight. I've

stopped dancing on my own. I've known
the nights, epidemics
to be shaken off.

SOUND/CHEST

CONSTITUTIONAL/BOUND   1719

As am I—try:
that's the way
these things end up ::
barking and hysterical and.
And the lights went
on for you and the
lights went out for
me. It was a digital
boy. And where light
wears on for you, it's
disgusted of me.

Now that I
kind of know how
you felt, on the floor
with your legs bare
and the music still undoing
the hem of your skirt, I am unable
to see these ascensions
in another way: our muscles

don't atrophy
because we ignore them
but because we get used to them—
we're alright with their
starvation. I am not an aphasiac
and these are not
my gestures.

We were able and un-
able and they
were screaming. I imagined
the streets had been
torn apart but never
thought about the falling
blocks of building. Our
houses were low
and away and were part
of the metadata. We knew
where to go and how to decide
that we were being saved and
they were being
punished. This is a vision
of forty-one years from now:
even priests are running
from the ruins and
our city is buried by the sea.
This is Lisbon but not now.
Everywhere the waves
are crashing down but
lighter and lighter still. Noise
(move to the next one).

Forget
my reliance
on your words—this junk is
entirely mine. Pails
are filling
graveyards on
my tongue, pale
and amorous
like religious
salts. Whatever's roasting
has little to wheeze.

My famine
is a victim of delight,
a private mass
for severed noise. The
grey wood skin
is marked for time:
my distance is waste
and I'm the only one
not at fault. This saturation
is about forgiveness
and speed is
rendered of
nightlines. The tones
left are shelved and
compressing.

ERRATIC/DISPOSABLE   1696

Whatever they're
wanting, we're not
smelting. These
cobwebs forming
are yours: they drape
themselves
on the corners,
at your face. My atrophy
is not for these people—
this is not about
the house or even
about the scars. I know
how to America.

I can only peel
myself away. All
this sand has to rush
somewhere again. Once
in the bushes, beat-
en, steal: what the
reading ended up
as being :: what
the rain said
to the cast. The
gift was so
we would become
safety deposits.

GRATITUDE/INTENTION   1724

Turn it
—next—
you're miss—

you're missing the beeps—

that was Johnny
Appleseed. I
don't believe
you or in
primordial
couch surfing. There's
a natural stop just

turn it
—now.

Welcome to my
hyperstability. I
haven't built this
bridge for migration: my
balance belongs
in a zoo. The land
has been salted
so we can maintain
the imbalance. All
diseases vetted,
our Kansas
is this ache.

PERMANENT/GRADATION   1747

As if the words around us
were waiting on our ears to
hear them:

                        the systems
already in place are there so
we don't starve, don't drown in
the flood that is increasingly
about us.

WET/FISTED   1691

You couldn't believe the hole
I put through the table: my knees
were the only indulgence I ever

gave myself. I bit at routine hard
and saw more of the strings than
I knew were there. The splinters

and the grains that were tearing
(I felt like ripping through with
my teeth and sucking dry the table)

and flaking and becoming the
floor. The names on the table were
etched and carefully considered.

Why is the letter opener so cold?
It went through and through in
time and the chessboard drawn

on the surface sank at the rook's
corner.

PORTFOLIO/EVIDENCE   1722

I've reached
the sulfur stage
of my gestation and
been sought after for
my anemic thoughts. As
the revolver spins, you
see the threads
dangle and shred.
We've become
a penetrative glance
more likely to
spit than talk
around. This word is
that word minus
a séance: welcome
to the language of teeth.
I've stolen all the
regrets I know about.

STUDY/KARMA

1706

This is the ocean life, the
way to sell the seeds
in back orders. All
that can be done
is about the rolling
of the most eyes: I've
been this torture before.
The scattered frames
remind you that I put
sprocket holes
in my head
so you could
turn forward at
the beeps. Each click
has become about
the weather and
not the change
gathering ashes.

SOUND/CHEST

ASHES/RETRIBUTION   1744

As it comes
together, the swerve
in the road
and the tiny outline
of motion that creates, resettles. We
are not the flashes of light
in these frames
but the darkness which fades
in the next minute.

After, the
bruises became
her thighs: the next
blooms. Rotten
flowers,
symbols of
sustainability. In photos
where she's
Joan of Arc,
I prefer the ones
with her glasses
taped and in
a purple dress. This
music plays
faster as she says
no and smiles.

TEXT/IMAGE   1684

What was asked about
in thunder was how
the tiles came up
and the ceilings
came down. An electrical
short circulates,
my bunny, jaundiced of
love. I saw this weak
flip coming and I
bought my handles in
red and glass.

This happened
to the covers: they
became the room. And
even in her gloom
she wondered at the
ceiling dripping paint
and egg whites. My mystery
in cashmere and everything
not mine, but I don't
know what I've stolen
from everyone else. Helltown,
Ohio is not
properly labeled
on the map but this room
could be an infinite metastization of
these facts that go
on the covers and burning. To
sleep goes the hiatus
and the imaginary light on
in the woods. I have been healing
through breathing: this
sacrifice void.

HIDE/RESULTS

Words we've never heard
are holding us back: sitting
on her couch realizing
her dog could swallow
my head. She was wearing
a coat and talking
about the rain
on a road trip and all
I could see was her tape
and sunglasses
on someone else's dashboard and
her hair in the wind
of someone else's vacation. There
was some talk of electrical
outlets and role-playing.

This is the office so
she leans forward
again. My washtub is
blood-spattered and raucous.
Even at night, I
can hear the fireworks
as they bounce off the
engraved faces. Elvis
wishes he were back
in time. My president has
a handle that lacks vision. In
the doorway I felt the brush
passed of a hand and two mice
racing the hands up and down:
these many aisles wavering
in sawdust. It's grainy
even when you've gone
over a dozen times and still
there are no songs you
remember hearing.

(THE) A/ANTIDOTE   1685

Suicide among the
daffodils: I've seen this
stage before. The furniture
in this room has been
stacked against
the ossuary. Murder a
phase I cannot
wake out of and
the steeping of
this village is testing
my knees. The trees
try to pretend
they hate the attention
and the span
of the trimmer's
arms. My crown
slips from
her gaze.

Us
at the table
and red: glasses
that don't
need tape. I see her
listening to jazz
and should have
said no. Plastic
forms the new
fever. I was from
Saturday and she was
Sunday breakfast. Tiles
are stuck and
germinating: your hoodie,
a nervous smile.

EVIL/ALERTNESS   1726

This isn't the last stop, just
the one best known when you
read nothing or imagine everything
around you is burning. It is this
paranoia which allows us to move on,
to pick out the known sayings in
our speech. Everything else is a
prayer that we keep for when
the moment comes that the wheel
must be turned. The drawers aren't
empty: they are lined with the
connections of our language. Just

the normal reverb in here that
belongs and makes sure we do,
too.

I went with an understanding
of knowing: whatever wakes in
us when we're thinking of a way
out seems to be the best way
to handle the last glances. The
belt buckles, the door is no
longer ajar and any weight that
could be expected is placed
into the hands of everyone
who is determined to remember,
to remind us of that our
language can fester even
when we ourselves are
hanging from the rafters. It is
not always the quiet ones that
surprise us, just the ones who
mobilize us.

We're good at
pretending to know
what we're doing
during the lean hours. He
carried tools and
fixed glasses, waiting
for a nerve to work
up. Even then, she
pretended to know
what was happening
and he waited for nothing.
I saw him later
at the door as her
cab pulled away and
never said anything and
never talked about it
after that, but I could tell. These
were the moments where we
meditated in the yard
and stood with our legs apart
and our hands up, pretending
to hold a vase or a child
as long as we
could. I'm pretty sure he
never

They're going to have to I have
some sense another is another this
is the worst birth you've ever had
I believe it was the garbage man
who told me about Karnataka memory
stings are wasting and I know this
is where they put it I cannot become
and I am this is how the sidewalk
ends this is how the sidewalk
this is not to know but to do and
I saw the furious marigold studs
Mars on point to Venus you think
you're so funny and satire is the
something something sinking
treasure get inoculated this is that
amnesty and a ribbon in her hair
teams of privateers there's a word
I used to call my own something like
honoria meta-cognitive.

HESITATION/WARNING   1734

On the corner, a door that swings
either way out and a flash,
a flash that signals nothing at
all, but a turnaround: the drowning
never seems to bother us about
the flood. We are dragged down, the noise
that pushes us along but our eyes
were anything other than
attached. As her hair spun through
the intersection, I imagined a
new paradigm in which her resistance
became the space around her. We
pretended not to see each other but
it turned out she was thousands of miles
away anyways.

Not always the dream that drives us,
but sometimes the terror of knowing
no dream will come. We may placate
ourselves in our pride, but ultimately
behind the projector is a place of failure:
no one chooses to be terrible, we just
are. This is the deep sea now, the one
that drowns us as we attempt to rip the
nails from our fingers and slowly we
come to understand that we are not
power ourselves, but the vision
of someone else's forgery. Our
senses are not the ones lying:
we cover anything which
can be seen up close, especially
if the figment can remain in
anyone else's line.

DIVORCE/MANAGE   1712

This sinking needs
an exit sign, my
dandy need girl. My
ostrich has taken flight
and the seats are covered
white. I remember very
little of this space, and
what's left has been
archived and shipped.
Every time we twisted
this way, I began to burn

inside and I know
you remember sitting on a
couch one evening with me
and not him. Another time, we
were so far apart that I could
only see your angry look by
squinting at you hard. We
ended up on your
kitchen floor so
many times and the
imprint of your textured
vinyl on my skull.

This is the worst way I know:
I had this memorized before,
so just turn it when—you're
missing—this finger or that
one—to a lawnmower I—
heard it like that I—no
go back to the one before
the jelly—you're the one who
spilled the paste—you're the
one who flushed the
piece of her hair band
and shat on the edge of the—
problem I have is with
her Father—you're missing
the beeps and we're
out of people with—
fingers.

This is when a
life is built of wax
and dried flower
petals, dead and
set to music. I
saw the sky had
become my
mistress and her
name is
annoyance. There
are no more little
answers than
there are half lies
and truths. My
midnight is
strapped to dust
and when he lean
rose I was

pretty, beaming.
If you want to
know why I did
what I did,
believe that light
can trip even the
fanciest of feet
into mishearing a
burglar. We are
in this corner
unwarranted and
documented as
death-bringers. It
was back when
the best place to
visit was locally

AMISH TRIVEDI   49

manufactured.
The best you can
do is put up your
hair.

SOUND/CHEST

Stained objects are sexualized
at her feet: I began
a clemency. The deliberate
steps to her door were
chains of glass. A trouble does not
brew in the sudden
orgasmic environment. This shuttle is not
spasmodic but I
settle on the floor in her overcoat
and palace. The crushed unveiling
of a letter in silence: a dream
that fools you into a real
kind of immolation. My disgrace
was an arrangement
out of wax. What I mean is
 "indulgent."

That there is something glorious
in this deposed place
is a myth. All these
things are the thoughts
I've had about you
today: sleeping late
on a Saturday morning
and having trouble
with outlets. If they move
anything else, this chair
will be renamed The Oceans.
This is where
the atlas went
and where the designs
came from

—and I never stopped—
I never began. And I never
would have left and
become eggs.

DISMEMBERMENT/FORGERY   1721

This is my pervasive nihilism
and I cannot speak
without looking down
anymore. The words
I use sometimes
are heard to be threats,
or, more often,
promises. This is standard
time, a beat

that replaces the one
in our throats with
lingering doubt. We
are being portrayed
as everything we are
and that scares me.

ABANDONMENT/OBSCURANT   1698

This was the day
for a smoke screen that
I had seen before. He
has returned
and there's no rebellion
to be found. I built this war
to reflect what I saw
in space: this war and
this well-rested night.
I saw all the lights flicker
multiple times
before questioning
the power generation. What-
ever and whatever, this
is the used up end and the
beginning that's waning.

FOIL/DOSE   1732

This is our last time around
with no sign
that we've been here
before. Next time,
I plan on leaving early
before they fuck us up
again. Asked about where
he was going, he always said
he was coming back
and smiled. This made them
cringe and pretend
they understood. He noted
the pained look
on their faces and wrote down
the time. There was an angelic baby
on her shoulder
and he was introduced as
the father. His face was the same
as theirs.

He kept himself
grounded as he worked
on the line because he knew
the dangers of power. One jolt
might not be so bad, he
would joke, but he knew
he'd be dead. And when he
was driving home and a woman
hit him from behind going
twice the speed limit, blinded
by the afternoon sun,
he made it home and cried
in my arms, amazed and sad
he was still alive. His seat fell
backwards and he was lying
down when they pulled him
out. She claimed his car
was just a dark blur at impact.

RELINQUISH/SEPARATE 1705

I had known where
to dig: this soil
is new. Being wrapped
up in the permutations
of an afternoon is no good
for anyone. She wished
she were there with someone,
out beneath the stars
and the lack of city lights
to block them. We were
looking billions of miles,
only to realize that the
light had come to us
and it was time to let go.
The cushion between us
was all the space
we needed as the heat
of a summer afternoon settled
over us and we knew
the time was not now. Two quick,
stoned tears
at the bottom of a
blank page.

There's a generic statement
they could make. I have
no mouth to speak of
or tones to speak with. The fists
have gambled with many a lock
and lost. I was told this generation
would be built for the
massacres ahead. If you saw
this permanent cloud, you'd
be wondering where the
hell the fog had gone. I got billed
for my own fantasy. Another
moment in the middle
of a movie where I could
have walked out or cried
myself to dungeons: I'm a
prisoner like a steel beam
holding these transoms. I was
going to be dead when I grew up,
or the answer to saturation.

INDUCTED/PROLONG   1707

In the middle
of a lean minute :: the
biopsy of a regular
work day. I
wish I were uglier
on the inside, then
you could justify
your fasting.

Sometimes
these echoes
are lost
in the walls
and anything
with skin has
absorbed
all the paints. When
we were pulling all
the dead things out, we
noticed how malformed
the earth was. It was set
to burn and set to while
away the hours. This mess
and that as part
of the whole: battle
lines are rubbed out.

GARNERED/IMAGES   1711

I got a hot minute
of decadence that'll
rip the enamel
off your teeth. These
self-pity shows
were popular before
they stopped being fun
as soon as I gained
an eye. The dangerous streets
are piling up with glass. I saw

this rebellion
in a movie once:
we were going to celebrate
Mardi Gras as a fort and would
have used a tuning fork
as well.

I'm pulling at
whatever
is left and
I don't
believe you anymore.
This is what
you get out of scraps
and and rewriting:
it's all over now. Sometimes
you don't feel
the need to turn
it or and or I know
this way. This is just
one manner of destruction
and another kind of leaf and
it needs burning. My needs are
melting and I can't hear
this train bearing down. I heard
about the cover up and left it alone.

INSIGNIFICANT/COIL   1695

This is the story I've heard
more than once.
You repeat it
whenever you get a chance
and I can't seem to stop
thinking about birds and
the flash. It's the wheel
I know that's broken
down and I can't stand up
anymore. Out from here
it's the radiation
that grows. My timing belt's flawed
and I just answered the door
as Eurydice, so don't look
back. Wherever they were headed,
it wasn't here, so we trick'd 'em
into thinking it was.

I cannot look at
photos of you. I
promised myself I
wouldn't. This was
the amount
that was prescribed to me
when I dug up the sand
and gently
laid my head down. You're
reacting to me and
in the background,
just to the side,
there's a momentary
glare. I don't imagine
you've witnessed
my disease. Even
in profile your stare
is nothing new.

TASTEFUL/ABDICATION 1680

Your new gaze reminds
me of an air I cannot
help but breathe: it's
the final suffocation that
means the most to me. Ultimately,
we're an affirmation
of all the things we've
said, the things that sting
which we cannot familiarize
ourselves with unless we reabsorb
our words in new arrangements. Your
enumerations are lusting
after my lettering.

I could spend these
hours blaming you
for not imagining
happy, but I imagine
the looks I used to get
when I ignored you: they
were lusty and bleached.
An old photo I tore up
reminded me of the days
before my confession,
stumbling naked across
the bathroom floor and
trying to remember why
I spat at the end of every
cigarette. I was acting
dumb again and you
bought it.

PERSONAGE/BRAIN   1692

I've stayed
awake, as
needed. The bruises best
when ripe,
the asphyxiation,
dark. This natural light
burns a hole
in my retina and
I've made up the bed with
wet dust. There are no
straight flowers any
more, only pills
that stopped sinking
to the bottom of the glass.

In desperation, we build
it better: the answers
are forthcoming. Our regret
cannot find us when we hide in
the frame, so we become the nitrate
and imagine a new life in every
scene. The repetition of our
peril brings us to artifice,
though we've known it
all along. This is the
dénouement and we're
breaking in again.

Leaping hearts are soaked
in formaldehyde: grey and
dead of roast beef ambitions.
Holding another person's
pump—another way of
guessing at traffic signals. My
murder is evangelical
in its ignorance. This is the
leverage I want: weak. About
the time the bulbs choked
the sunlight off, I began a
sweet style of defamation. These words
are all the same
and wooden. Easily tossed
and empty. Searching does not
mean finding.

What was a face is
now a wreck
of defiance, mangled
and debt
accumulating. These days
I'm feeling more stranded
and burdened with
knives. My favorite emotion
is chloroform, bagged and
ignored out

by the wolves and
traffic. The next trick
will be an illustration of
security. A mantra is a noise,
black and nihilistic like
lungs across
the rapid fire
regeneration. My love is
caught and mulling: the twenties
are a way of spelling
napalm and majesty. I was the one
who knew the angles of the roof.

Another hook, daringly
ended: the kid in your arms
looks as trapped as I am by
the memory of us having spoken
once. You were polite, but
there was no way to not
feel bruised about it. It was a
hot moment and I wasn't
about anything specific. Sometimes
we just memorize the things we
want to say so no one
can forgive us.

CORD/FUEL   1699

There are only things
to miss about an ostrich: my
dandy need girl
—garden end
idyl. That which
is pulled and
set for
destruction is
a landing re-dyed.

The pieces I know
are rabid
as rust, an inevitable
suffering.

I used to hear
stories about
cheap drinks and
lunchtimes spent in
trysts: everything here
is damaged water.

I can go on pretending. I am
the denial I wish to be in
the world. The water will
not drown me as I am of
this flood, I am of this
plain. The water will
not flood me as I am
this river's course and I
am its mouth and its delta. The
headwaters are around me and
I kind of like it.

GENIUS/OPTIMIST   1740

I waited all day
because I knew

"this is how I think."

I won't
ring the bell
and they are
watching me. These
are the indicators
as far as I know:
marshmallows
and paraffin wax.
I was told
I'd never need to worry:
this is what monotony
always sounded like.

AFTER/WORD

The titles to these poems come from labels on a discarded card catalog that I found while wandering around the basement at the University of Iowa's Main Library in June of 2008. There were several cabinets that were being prepared to go to surplus, and while normally I paid no attention to them, the fact that this one cabinet still had labels drew my eye.

While there is probably no way of knowing exactly what the catalog's function was, a librarian's best guess is that they were used for a custom filmstrip collection. What the words and numbers are in relation to has been lost. The filmstrip, though, is that archaic bit of grade school technology that required the teacher to assign a student to turn a knob when the supplemental audio urged her to do so, usually through the use of an annoying beep that caused the inattentive turner to startle and flip the knob quickly but always too late.

My goal was to create a relationship between these words and in most cases, the numbers. Our minds, through the use of language, create relationships between ideas all the time, and I felt that with such a diverse set of ideas existing in one collection, there was little to do but manufacture that relationship.

The card catalog intrigues me with its ability to be fascinating and useless at the same time. Language is ultimately ephemeral in that it is always changing and never static. Language must be treated with a movement towards levity, as it is always light with us. Numbers seem random and scattered in these poems; they often function as years, referring to the fleeting nature of history.

SOUND/CHEST

Unfortunately, around the time of the floods in the summer of 2008, while the rest of the library's basement contents were moved to higher floors, the card catalog cabinet was emptied of its labels and most likely moved to surplus for sale. The only record of these titles and numbers now are these poems.

ACKNOWLEDGEMENTS

Poems from *Sound/Chest* have appeared in *Cannibal* (Clustered/Brain 1728, Ritual/Abstinence 1736, His/Empty 1737), *Golden Handcuffs Review* (Desirous/Actions 1729, Genius/Optimist 1740), *Open Letters Monthly* (Portfolio/Evidence 1722) and *Pismire* (1717, Truncated/Obvious 1713), where the text is paired with audio. Other poems have been featured on Jerome Rothenberg's Jacket2 Commentary/Blog, Poems & Poetics, (Dose/Farewell 1738, Combine/Liquid 1735, Sound/Syllable 1708, Attempts/Unrealized 1718, Abandonment/Obscurant 1698 Foil/Dose 1732, Factory/Shadow 1725), along with a previous version of the After/Word. Thanks to Matt Henriksen, Lou Rowan, Ezekiel Black, Maureen Thorson, and Jerome Rothenberg.

Thanks to Joshua Edwards, Lynn Xu, and everyone else at Canarium Books for naming *Sound/Chest* a finalist back in 2010.

A special thanks to the University of Iowa Libraries, specifically to Janalyn Moss and Sandra Ballasch for their help in finding out more about this abandoned and mysterious card catalog. Thanks as well to a wonderful set of student employees for their support of my curiosity and the work that emerged from it. Also thanks to Dee Morris, in whose class I began work on the manuscript, and to the incredibly kind students in that course, especially Michelle Taransky Kleiman, Robert Fernandez, and Mary Hickman. Thanks to Christopher Merrill and Natasa Durovicova, who allowed me to sit in on the International Writing Program's Friday afternoon translation workshops.

SOUND/CHEST

Further thanks to Jessica Smith, Gillian Devereux, François Luong, Michelle Detorie, and Michalle Gould; to Forrest Gander (for his line by line additions, deletions and corrections that found their way into the manuscript), C.D. Wright, Keith and Rosmarie Waldrop, and Brian Evenson; to Claire Donato, Adam Veal, Darren Angle, Mark Baumer, Andrew Bourne, Rachel Cole Dalamangas, Christopher Sweeney, Robert Snyderman, and many other classmates in Brown University's Literary Arts Program for their comments and notes; to Gale Nelson, Lori Baker, Johannes Göransson, Joyelle McSweeney, Kate Schapira, Kate Colby, Darcie Dennigan, Catherine Imbriglio, Edward J. Delaney, Adam Braver, Diane Rothenberg, David Smith, Bobby Wesley, the McLoones and Mattes, my parents, Dinendra and Kamakshi, my brother Arpit and his family, my in-laws, Peter and Jean, various siblings-in-law, aunts, uncles, cousins and, especially, Jennifer.

ABOUT THE AUTHOR

Amish Trivedi's poems are in *New American Writing, The Laurel Review, CutBank, Mandorla, XCP, Cannibal, Golden Handcuffs Review* and various other locations. His chapbooks include *Everyone's But Mine* (Paradigm Press, 2014), *Museum of Vandals* (Cannibal Books, 2009), and *Selections from Episode III* (Beard of Bees, 2009). His reviews have been in *Jacket2, Sink*, and *Pleiades*. He is the managing editor of *N/A* (www.nalitjournal.com) and lives with his wife Jennifer in Providence, Rhode Island where he teaches at Roger Williams University.

CPSIA information can be obtained at www.ICGtesting.com
Printed in the USA
BVOW05s1321120315

391403BV00002B/3/P

9 780692 346266